LEARNING
TO LEAD

LEARNING TO LEAD

Pat Heim and Elwood N Chapman

KOGAN
PAGE

First published in the United States of America
in 1990 by Crisp Publications Inc, 95 First Street,
Los Altos, California 94022, USA.

This edition first published in Great Britain in
1991 by Kogan Page Ltd, 120 Pentonville Road,
London N1 9JN.

British Library Cataloguing in Publication Data

A CIP record for this book is available from the British Library.

ISBN 0-7494-0568-6

Typeset by DP Photosetting, Aylesbury, Bucks
Printed and bound in Great Britain by
Clays Ltd, St Ives plc

Contents

To the Reader

What would you prefer to be called? An excellent manager or an excellent leader? Maybe you haven't considered the differences between the two, but most people would rather be designated an excellent leader because it suggests a quality that goes beyond basic management skills.

The purpose of this book is to enhance your present management abilities with a stronger, more discernible dimension. In short, this book was developed to help sharpen your leadership skills. It assumes you are already familiar with what it takes to become a good manager. As most leaders recognise, it is necessary to become a capable manager before one will be regarded as a good leader.

Solid management skills provide the foundation upon which to build a leadership dimension. These skills remain essential during the leadership building process. Also, after becoming a leader, you must *maintain* your management competencies. It is the combination of both management and leadership skills that will provide the formula for your success.

Do most managers possess the basic ability to become leaders? Yes, but only if their desire is sufficiently intense. Such a challenge requires behavioural changes. These can only be made with hard work and repetition. It is therefore suggested that you read this book in its entirety before deciding the level of commitment you are willing to make.

If you decide to initiate a leader/manager improvement programme, you will want to follow the advice presented on a page-by-page basis. Taken seriously, the contents of this book constitute a powerful programme that produces positive results. The decision is yours.

Pat Heim
Elwood N Chapman

About This Book

Learning to Lead is not like most books. It has a unique self-paced format that encourages a reader to become personally involved. Designed to be 'read with a pencil', there is an abundance of exercises, activities, assessments and cases that invite participation.

The objective of *Learning to Lead* is to provide the fundamentals of both good management *and* leadership skills.

Learning to Lead (and the other titles in the Better Management Skills series) can be used effectively in a number of ways. Here are some possibilities:

● *Individual study*. Because the book is self-instructional, all that is needed is a quiet place, some time and a pencil. By completing the activities and exercises, a reader will not only receive valuable feedback, but also practical steps for self-improvement.

● *Workshops and seminars*. This book is ideal as assigned reading prior to a workshop or seminar. With the basics in hand, the quality of the participation will improve and more time can be spent on concept extensions and applications during the programme. The book is also effective when it is distributed at the beginning of a session, and participants 'work through' the contents.

● *Distance learning*. Books can be sent to those unable to attend head office training sessions.

There are many other possibilities that depend on the objectives, programme or ideas of the user.

One thing is certain. Even after this book has been read, it will be looked at – and thought about – again and again.

CHAPTER 1
What is Your Leadership Potential?

Leadership potential scale

If you expect to become a manager or already occupy a managerial position, you may wonder whether or not you have the potential to lead others. This exercise is designed to help you reach this decision. Read the statement at both ends of the scale and then circle the number that best indicates where you belong. Most people fall somewhere between the two extremes.

	High	**Low**
I can be both an excellent manager and have time to lead.	10 9 8 7 6 5 4 3 2 1	I am satisfied being a good manager.
I am a visionary. I love to plan for long-term goals.	10 9 8 7 6 5 4 3 2 1	Getting by one day at a time is my goal.
Risk-taking is my cup of tea. It challenges me.	10 9 8 7 6 5 4 3 2 1	I avoid risks whenever possible.
It is a challenge to discipline others.	10 9 8 7 6 5 4 3 2 1	I do not enjoy having to discipline others.
I enjoy communication and have the potential to become outstanding.	10 9 8 7 6 5 4 3 2 1	My communication skills are adequate.

	High	Low
I have the desire to become a top leader.	10 9 8 7 6 5 4 3 2 1	I'm comfortable as a follower.
I enjoy making difficult decisions.	10 9 8 7 6 5 4 3 2 1	Decisions can be frustrating and scary.
I seek and welcome more responsibility.	10 9 8 7 6 5 4 3 2 1	I avoid added responsibilities.
I can handle the pressure of being under fire and in the limelight.	10 9 8 7 6 5 4 3 2 1	Pressure is not for me.
I believe I have the personality to become a successful leader.	10 9 8 7 6 5 4 3 2 1	Sorry, I'm not the leadership type.

Total ☐

If you scored 80 or above, it would appear that you have a high desire and potential to be a leader. A rating between 60 and 80 shows good potential. A rating under 60 is a signal that you may wish to delay weaving leadership practices into your management style.

Differences between managers and leader/managers

Explaining the differences between managers and leaders can be difficult. Recognising this, the following statements may help you to distinguish your dimensions of leadership. Please tick the appropriate box depending on whether you agree or disagree with the following statements:

Agree   Disagree

☐   ☐   A good manager is content simply to follow directions and suggestions from above. A leader/manager is more apt to consider the future and anticipate needs, problems and issues before being told that action is needed.

☐   ☐   A good manager is willing to accept responsibility. A leader/manager seeks responsibility.

☐   ☐   An effective manager will take modest risks (when the odds are favourable). A leader/manager accepts higher risks when they have the potential to result in greater progress, and commits to a plan of action with greater determination.

☐   ☐   A leader/manager has more of an entrepreneurial spirit than a basic manager.

☐   ☐   A manager is more apt to accept comfortable assignments while a leader looks for more demanding opportunities to demonstrate his or her leadership potential.

☐   ☐   A manager usually views those under his or her supervision as employees. A leader views employees as team members and followers.

Agree   Disagree

☐   ☐   A basic difference between managers and
                    leaders is attitude. Many managers are
                    content to set modest goals, pacify others,
                    try for a comfortable working
                    environment and use power cautiously. A
                    leader tends to set more demanding goals,
                    challenges others and creates a more
                    dynamic working environment.

If you ticked 'Agree' on all boxes, you should find that the ideas
presented in this book will be comfortable to practise and
incorporate in your daily activities.

Are only sound managers free to lead?

Leadership at any level is built on basic management skills. Until
an operation is well managed, the person in charge is not
sufficiently free to lead. Thus those attempting to lead without
fundamental management competencies usually fail before they
get started.

'You can't lead an organisation if you are constantly putting out
management-related fires.'

'Some weeks it is all I can do to act as a caretaker around here.
Lead? You must be joking.'

'I feel apologetic about the fact that I can free myself to lead only
now and then.'

A few individuals are in a high enough position to select and train
good administrative personnel who can free them to lead. But a
first level manager who desires to lead must learn to manage
efficiently in such a way that she or he has the freedom to add the

leadership dimension to their style. This means that managers who want to lead must free themselves by learning to be:

- Superior teachers, counsellors and delegators
- Outstanding time managers who are good at setting priorities and establishing goals
- Excellent system and control developers and operators.

What are the dangers of reaching into leadership before excellent management practices are in position?

It is possible to wind up in limbo and lose your management job.

Confusing leadership with management skills can leave you (the would-be leader) frustrated.

Employees can feel insecure or lose respect for the way you operate.

First things first. Hone your management skills before jumping into leadership situations.

CHAPTER 2
Is Leadership for You?

Making a leadership commitment

Not everyone aspires to lead. Some capable, valuable individuals are content to be excellent managers. These people prefer the recognition that comes from good management techniques. They leave visionary risks to others. At a certain point in their careers they would rather 'follow' as a manager than lead others from a more demanding position. Their management position gives them all the leadership responsibility they desire or need.

What about you?

Listed below are three major reasons why most managers elect to improve their leadership potential. Read each statement and tick the box that most accurately reflects your feelings.

	Exactly how I feel	Partly how I feel	Not how I feel
1. I seek more personal fulfilment than I can achieve in a management role. I want to feel I have improved the destiny of my organisation. I am afraid I will get lost in the crowd if I don't step out of a pure management position.	☐	☐	☐

	Exactly how I feel	Partly how I feel	Not how I feel
2. As a manager, I feel boxed in. I want freedom to make more decisions and more power to execute them. Taking more risks will keep me motivated and I will be more likely to reach my full potential as a person.	☐	☐	☐
3. I want upward mobility. I want to climb the executive ladder higher and faster. Money is important, but even more important is my desire to achieve some really meaningful long-term goals.	☐	☐	☐

Invitation to a three-step challenge

Step 1. Carefully complete the management assessment scale on the opposite page.

Step 2. While reading this book, try to keep the differences between a successful manager and a leader clear in your mind.

Step 3. Complete the management leadership assessment scale on page 67 and compare it with your score on page 21.

Management assessment scale

This survey describes 20 practices that are common to excellent managers. Read all the statements carefully. Then decide as a present or future manager the priority you would assign each practice or characteristic. Indicate your decision by circling the appropriate number.

	Highest	**High**	**Important**	**Modest**	**Low**
			PRIORITY		
1. Strives to keep employees fully informed.	5	4	3	2	1
2. Expresses thoughts clearly.	5	4	3	2	1
3. Good listener.	5	4	3	2	1
4. Shows compassion.	5	4	3	2	1
5. Provides important rewards for staff.	5	4	3	2	1
6. Wins by allowing employees also to win.	5	4	3	2	1
7. Has full backing from those under him/her.	5	4	3	2	1
8. Provides structure to create cohesive feeling.	5	4	3	2	1
9. Establishes consistent, clear discipline lines.	5	4	3	2	1
10. Gets tough when needed.	5	4	3	2	1
11. Respected by employees when authority is used.	5	4	3	2	1
12. Uses power with sensitivity.	5	4	3	2	1
13. Consults others in making decisions.	5	4	3	2	1
14. Follows logical steps in making decisions.	5	4	3	2	1
15. Admits to mistakes.	5	4	3	2	1
16. Maintains positive, upbeat attitude.	5	4	3	2	1
17. Makes work enjoyable.	5	4	3	2	1
18. Shares large and small victories with staff.	5	4	3	2	1
19. Delegates effectively.	5	4	3	2	1
20. Highly ethical in all situations.	5	4	3	2	1

TOTAL SCORE

Later in this book you will be invited to prioritise these management characteristics along with 20 leadership practices. This unique process will help you to differentiate between management and leadership skills. It will also provide insight into the future role you desire for yourself.

CHAPTER 3
Developing Your Leadership Power Sources

Everyone has unused personality power

Personality power is the development and use of your best traits to influence others. It is being the best you can be – *on a personal basis*. When you hear someone say, 'My manager motivates us' you are hearing a message about the power of a positive personality. Everyone has a unique personality that can be transmitted effectively to others. Some individuals may be blessed with more power than others, but all of us possess more power than we realise. And it is not how much power we have, but rather how we use it.

Personality power is expressed through both physical *and* mental traits. Personality power is transmitted when people make the most of their *best* traits. They have learned to isolate these special traits that impress others and concentrate on improving and transmitting them. In this way, they learn to increase their personality power.

Personality power is important to leaders. Without personality power followers would not be inspired to reach for new goals. Leaders must use their power to *influence*. They generate as much personality power as possible and use it wisely. The purpose of Chapter 1 is to help you develop your personality power.

Play up your best traits

Not too long ago, psychologists and management experts believed it took a special combination of personality traits (distinguishing characteristics) to become a successful leader. No one, however, was able to prove what many people started to call the Trait Theory. Today, experts agree that there are so many acceptable traits – in so many combinations and mixes – that virtually everyone has a degree of personality power. In other words, you are not disqualified as a potential leader if you wear glasses, are unusually tall or prefer to read books rather than work out in a health club.

To become a successful leader, however, you *do* need to identify and develop a mix of your best traits and then learn to communicate them effectively. This is the major challenge you face as you commit yourself to putting more leadership into your management style. Ask yourself these questions:

Can I recognise and communicate my best physical charac-
    teristics?
Is there room for improvement in my verbal skills?
Do I have some good mental traits that I should feature and
    communicate more frequently?
What role should attitude play in my personality power
    package?

The route to take if you wish to have more influence over others is to emphasise your special, distinguishable traits. Do not be over-concerned with personal traits you would prefer to be different – simply identify, improve and transmit your best traits. For example, if you have attractive hair, make the most of it. If you have more patience than others, use this trait to gain compliments. If you have a full, authoritative voice, use it to your advantage. In other words, *play your winners!*

Three sources of leadership power

1. Personality power
To understand the potential of your personality power, it is necessary to appreciate two other primary sources, role power and knowledge power. The illustration opposite gives personality power the biggest segment, but it would be a mistake to underestimate the possible power of the other two.

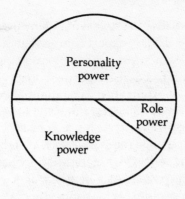

What are other power sources?

2. Role power
Role power comes from the position you hold. This is not power that comes from knowledge or experience. It is not power that comes from your personality traits. Role power goes with your position regardless of who occupies it. The moment someone is promoted into the role of supervisor, he or she gains power. We have all witnessed the abuse of role power, even at the lowest level.

3. Knowledge power
Knowledge power comes from understanding the skills and techniques required for effective behaviour in a given role. As our society becomes increasingly technical and roles become more specialised, knowledge power becomes more and more important.

When someone decides to work to build up their skills, power sources come quickly into play. When this happens, the following considerations surface:

- How can one make sensitive use of all power sources?
- When is it best to draw power from one source as opposed to another?
- How does one achieve the perfect or best balance in the daily use of all three sources?

These, and other questions, will be answered on the following pages.

Play down your role power

As a manager you have been given some authority over others. Those above you may have more power, but this does not diminish what you have received. As a leader, however, you may improve your value to the organisation by assuming you have slightly more role power. As a new manager you must still play down your role power in comparison with that of your other two sources.

You are the designated 'boss' so you lead the team. But keep in mind that without the role, your power may not yet be established. This means you will want to make the best possible use of role power but be humble enough to recognise that no matter who occupies the role, *the power is still there*. Role power is a temporary franchise. With this in mind, *agree* or *disagree* with the following statements by ticking the appropriate box.

Agree   Disagree

☐   ☐   A true leader does not need to remind team members that he or she is in charge.

☐   ☐   The more effectively you use knowledge and personality power, the less you will need to use role power.

☐   ☐   The best use of role power is to maintain discipline. Sometimes it must be used to restore structure so that all can reach their productivity potential.

☐   ☐   It is possible to communicate your role power through your actions and activities.

☐   ☐   When people respect you as a person they are more likely to respect the role you occupy.

Agree   Disagree

☐   ☐   When someone says, 'The new supervisor's job has gone to his or her head', the individual means that role power is being abused.

☐   ☐   It is not easy to live with newly acquired role power, especially at the beginning.

☐   ☐   Leaders who seek more role power must learn to use it in a sensitive manner at the very beginning.

Play up your knowledge power

Many managers and leaders foolishly play down knowledge as a power source. Knowledge power may be the safest and best way to demonstrate leadership. Reflect for a moment on why most people respect mentors. Isn't it because the mentor provides knowledge and guidance? If you agree, then you should strive to be both a mentor and a leader to your staff. In other words, be an outstanding *teacher*. Share your knowledge. Take time to give instructions in a clear and complete manner. Turn your employees into followers by using knowledge to build a better relationship with them.

With the above in mind, *agree* or *disagree* with the following statement by ticking the appropriate box.

Agree   Disagree

☐   ☐   Leaders need to be more sensitive to and generous in sharing their knowledge.

☐   ☐   Of the three sources, knowledge power is the best way to earn respect from a staff member.

Agree	**Disagree**	
☐	☐	The more you know about your job or business, the more knowledge power you have. Translated, this means the best use of knowledge power is to continue to learn.
☐	☐	It is possible to overuse knowledge power and wind up being viewed as a know-all.
☐	☐	Your personality power is the best way to communicate your knowledge power.
☐	☐	One need not be as sensitive in the use of knowledge power as of role power.
☐	☐	Most managers and leaders have more knowledge power than they realise, thus they tend to underuse it.
☐	☐	Practical experience is an excellent way to gain more knowledge power.

Capitalise on your different physical traits

When you ask someone to name a leader, you may be surprised. The leader may have an image far different from what you anticipated. This may be because leaders sometimes recognise the importance of emphasising their distinguishing features. These features may not always fit normal expectations. Some leaders are short (Napoleon). Some have big noses (De Gaulle). Some disregard traditional grooming standards (Lincoln).

Most leaders, however, command attention. Think of the bearing displayed by tribal chieftains. Compare historical leaders such as Einstein, Churchill or Mother Teresa. All make the most of a few physical traits that are unattractive in the traditional sense.

Ask yourself this question: 'If I strengthen one or more of my unusual features, will it communicate more personality power than if I try to improve some of my less noticeable traits?' In most cases the answer is yes. Followers want their leaders to be different. They want their leaders to stand out. They do not ask their leaders to win beauty contests.

Listed below are ten physical characteristics. Identify the three that you feel distinguish you most from other people. To do this, simply circle the appropriate words. If you have a different trait (not listed), add it in the space provided.

EYES	SIZE
HAIR/BEARD	GROOMING
POSTURE/FIGURE	COMPLEXION
SMILE	GENERAL IMAGE
FACIAL EXPRESSION	OTHER _____
BEARING	

If you are interested in communicating a more serious 'leadership image' than in the past, consider highlighting the features you circled. Not only will people accept you more easily, but you will feel more comfortable with yourself. This, in turn, will give you more self-confidence.

More confidence equals more personality power!

Feature your best mental traits

It is more difficult to pinpoint strong mental characteristics than to recognise physical traits. Yet, as a leader, it is important to be known to have a few unusual traits that followers appreciate.

Listed overleaf are some mental characteristics that help followers to feel more secure. Circle the three that you feel are the strongest in your personal inventory. Or if you prefer, circle the three that you respect most and want to strengthen in the future.

PATIENCE	ABILITY TO TAKE PRESSURE
INTEGRITY	
TACT	BOUNCE-BACK ABILITY
COURAGE	WILLINGNESS TO ACCEPT RESPONSIBILITY
MEMORY	DETERMINATION
DISCIPLINE	WILLINGNESS TO TAKE RISKS
DECISIVENESS	
FAIRNESS	POSITIVE ATTITUDE
CONSISTENCY	OTHER _____

You have now selected three of your different mental traits. Three that stand out as values or standards in your behavioural patterns. Of course, *all* the mental traits will help you to become a better leader, but the idea is to be known to have a few that are outstanding. One way to accomplish this is to *play up* the three you selected without neglecting the others. In doing this, be true to yourself. For example, if you selected decisiveness, consistency and willingness to accept responsibility, it would work to your advantage if people recognised these qualities in you and talked about them openly in making an evaluation of your leadership abilities.

People find it easier to accept an individual as their leader when they recognise valued mental traits and standards.

Cultivate a more authoritative voice

Some years back, an author of this book interviewed 60 recognised leaders and made a point of asking this question: 'What helped you most to become a leader?' Almost half replied that their public speaking ability provided the greatest assistance.

Have you taken time to listen to your voice recently? If not, why not tape your voice and play it back from either a recorder or telephone answering device. Is it dull or vibrant? Draggy or crisp? Strong or weak? Choice of words is important, but the *way* you say words (diction) is also significant. It may inspire you to know that Eleanor Roosevelt took elocution lessons as First Lady of the United States and wound up as its representative to the United Nations, where her voice was heard around the world.

It is possible to train your voice to be clear, strong and decisive. A strong voice will help you to put more authority into your message and will communicate more leadership. This single trait is only one feature, but *it can make a difference*. If you are confident in your voice, you will be more confident speaking to groups and this confidence will be apparent in all your communications.

Here are some simple suggestions to improve your speaking abilities:

- If you desire to improve your abilities as a speaker, consider taking a course or join a speakers' organisation, such as Toastmasters.
- Believe in what you are saying.
- Avoid using 'non-words' such as uhhh or ummm.
- Refrain from making excuses or qualifying what you say with 'ifs' and 'maybes'.
- Except in cases where a tough situation is being faced and a line is being drawn, keep a smile on your face and communicate a positive attitude.
- Learn not to talk too much. Recognise that it is not how much you say, but what the listener hears and accepts.
- Balance everything you say by also being a good listener.
- Read *How to Communicate Effectively* or *Effective Presentation Skills* in the same series as this book.

Train your voice to put more power into your personality.

Discover your own brand of charisma

Charisma is a certain charm, a divinely conferred power. It can be defined as 'psychological attraction'. Charisma causes others to react to a person in a more positive way than would normally be the case. Sometimes, by emphasising our 'different traits', we can create a 'charisma' that was not previously discernible. More often charisma is the result of natural selection – that is, a few special traits blended together in our personality make-up.

Is personality the same as charisma? Not exactly. Personality consists of *all* the physical and mental characteristics of an individual that are transmitted as images to another person. Charisma occurs when a mix of a few attractive characteristics 'blend together' to create a special charm.

Do all leaders have charisma? No. Most leaders, in fact, recognise that they do not have charisma but, nevertheless, make the most of their personalities. In a short, informal survey many of those responding suggested that only about 10 per cent of leaders had charisma. This does not mean that charisma is not desirable. It is. But most leaders know they can develop the personality power required to be effective without having charisma.

When successful managers decide to stress leadership, they are wise to play up their best physical and mental characteristics (be the best they can with what they possess) and not be concerned with whether or not the changes they make will make them charismatic. As shown in the following sections of this book, leadership is much more than personality.

Don't underestimate the magic of your positive attitude

Few would disagree that attitude is the most significant and powerful characteristic in anyone's personality inventory. A positive, vibrant attitude is often the ingredient that highlights all other favourable traits. A positive attitude is necessary to project a winning leadership image – charismatic or not. A positive attitude is recognised as the 'magic' that transmits the best of anyone's personality. A negative attitude closes the door.

Attitude is simply the way you view the world around you. It is a perceptual or mental phenomenon. It is your focus on life. In a sense, you see what you want to see. If you concentrate on negative factors (and there are plenty) you will eventually wind up with a negative attitude. When you concentrate on positive factors, you are more apt to stay positive. It sounds easy when you say 'look on the bright side', but, of course, it isn't. A positive attitude can be everyone's most priceless possession.* To a leader it is essential.

Attitude is also the way you look at yourself. If you see yourself as a successful manager, the chances are that you will be one. If you also see yourself as a successful leader, it is more likely to occur. Consider these possibilities:

- When you are positive, all around you are positively influenced.
- A positive attitude converts a personality that is easy to ignore into one that isn't.
- A leader with a negative attitude doesn't keep followers for long.
- People reach their personality potential when they have a positive attitude.
- Individuals are more creative when they are positive.
- A positive attitude releases the enthusiasm stored up inside individuals – as a result, they have more confidence to play out their roles as leaders.

Case Study 1
Selecting the best available model

Crystal devoted the first few months following her promotion to becoming an excellent manager. She read extensively and took all available seminars on management-related topics. She applied techniques and principles alike. Her superiors were more than pleased with her performance.

During this period, Crystal based her behaviour on that of a manager who turned out to be a mentor. Then it occurred to her that the managers in her mentor's department were not promoted into leadership roles. Why was that? After talking to others and thinking it through, Crystal decided that her 'model' had not demonstrated enough leadership. He was a solid manager, but did not take the risks necessary to become a leader.

As a result, Crystal switched models. She discovered Ms Crane, who was both a strong leader and manager. Crystal became more visible and more decisive in her communications. She used all three of her power sources. In talking it over with her husband, Crystal said, 'I just decided that I had to start acting like a leader if I wanted future upward mobility'.

Is this typical of a situation in your organisation? Are excellent managers often left in their roles? Is it necessary to become a leader/manager to gain upward mobility? Defend your position in the space below and then compare your answer with those of the authors on page 74.

_____

_____

_____

_____

_____

Summary

Naturally, the more personality power you develop, the stronger your role as a leader can be. You will be able to communicate better. You will be more convincing when you ask others to accept your vision. Your stronger personality will help you to convert more employees into followers.

But it is not always how much power you have. More important is how you employ it. Sensitivity to others is the key! And sensitivity is facilitated when personality power is balanced with both role power and knowledge power. Many variables are involved.

- A leader with great knowledge can be effective even with a minimum of personality power.

- A leader who plays down role power and makes the most of his or her knowledge power can be effective with only modest personality power.
- A leader with little role power, and in a position where knowledge power is not highly important, is dependent upon personality power.

In summary, the following suggestions are made:

- Everyone has a few features (often physical) that others appreciate. Play your winners!
- Strive to develop all the best mental traits that are expected in leaders, but concentrate on a few that are most important to you so they will be talked about in a favourable light by others.
- Be proud of your personality and keep in mind that those who do not transmit their personalities effectively often look better to themselves than they do to others.
- Use the magic of a positive attitude to enhance your personality.
- Use caution in selecting the best possible leadership model.

CHAPTER 4
Develop a Vision

Leaders know where they are going

Think of the leaders you admire and you will usually find something unique about them. Great leaders inspire people to follow rather than just 'look after the shop'. Status quo is not enough: leaders are on the move, improving, growing and expanding into new areas.

What further distinguishes leaders is that their growth has a direction. Leaders know where they are going. As a follower, you might be breaking new ground with your leader. The process is exciting. A key ingredient is that leaders have a vision to which they are drawn.

To be a true leader, you must have a sense of what's important, how you can contribute, and make your mark. What do you value and how can you make those values contribute in a larger sense? If your ultimate aims are based upon self-interest, employees are not going to be highly motivated to go that extra mile. On the other hand, if your team can see how your direction can make a difference, their energy and focus will support your goals.

At times managers will say, 'There is no way I can shape my department. That's done by those above me.' In the end, however, it is either create your future or let others do it. Recall the leaders you admire. They didn't accept the status quo. The chances are that they pushed, nudged and changed the way things were previously done.

Once you begin to get a picture of your larger goal or vision, you can begin to plan strategy. The focus is more on the 'how' rather than the 'what'. A word of warning. In the past decade or two, we have glorified quantitative decision-making. This has led some to concentrate a disproportionate amount of attention on the correct calculations. Your vision cannot be determined with a calculator or a case study. It must be what matters most to you. There are no rights or wrongs when it comes to a vision, just what is passionately important to you.

Case Study 2
Too much attention to detail?

Barbara has always taken a great deal of professional pride in her accounting skills. She was a top student at college and has excelled in her job. In recognition of her performance, Barbara was promoted to accounts manager.

Barbara's attention to detail was always one of her greatest assets. Now that she is in management, the details of her position have increased tenfold, and she feels as if she is drowning. Her greatest asset has become a liability!

To sort out what is involved, Barbara has tried making lists. But there aren't enough hours to deal with everything on her lists. To make matters worse, her boss has begun to ask questions about where she's 'taking her department' and what her 'focus' is.

Barbara is beginning to wonder if she is really cut out for leadership. Is there any hope?

Write out your response below and compare it with that found on page 74.

See the patterns – delegate the details

To truly lead a group, you must not lose sight of the long view. You need to see the patterns, trends and opportunities rather than get caught up in the details, particularly when these immediate details loom as roadblocks. If you are true to your dream, your roadblocks will become hurdles.

Some strategies for staying focused

1. *No details until 10.00 am.* Many managers work best in the morning, but often find that this time is consumed by small issues. To concentrate on their larger goals, some set a rule that they are not to be interrupted and no meetings are to be scheduled until 10.00 am. During this time, they shut their doors and get the bulk of their serious work underway.

2. *Your top six.* Mary Kay Ashe, Chief Executive Officer of Mary Kay Cosmetics, focuses her thoughts at the end of each day. Before she leaves work, she writes down the six most important activities for the next day. When she comes in the next morning, these six items are handled first, before she gets caught up in daily details.

3. *Assess your focus.* Think about yesterday. What percentage of your time was spent moving towards your vision and long-term goals, and what percentage dealt with the daily drama of life? Balance is the key!

Where are decisions taking your department?

Make sure you take the long view, particularly in important decisions. It is important for you as a leader to demonstrate focus and consistency. Underlying these qualities are your values, and how you see yourself contributing to your department, organisation or industry. For example, regardless of responsibility, a leader wants a product with the most integrity, the highest quality, the safest reputation, the most dependability, etc. In other words, the desire to be the best is a passion.

This value focus drives decisions. There is no compromise. As a leader you may need to sacrifice a short-term goal to stay true to your vision. Do it! Nothing is more important than the big picture.

Consistency in where you are leading your followers is extremely important. Employees find it hard to keep up that extra level of motivation if decisions indicate they are headed one way today and another direction tomorrow. The consistency of your decisions signals your commitment to what you believe to be important.

Following is an excellent summary of a decision process.

---

1. Make the best decision you can – *by doing it* – and then observe your results.
2. Avoid 'perfection paralysis'. Everything you do won't be perfect, but if you start with a 'rough draft' and then shape and improve things as you go, you'll end up fine. Keep the big picture in mind.
3. Use a decision guide like the one illustrated below.

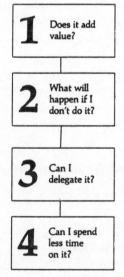

1	Does it add value?
2	What will happen if I don't do it?
3	Can I delegate it?
4	Can I spend less time on it?

Source: Reproduced with permission from *Successful Self-Management* by Paul R Timm (Kogan Page)

Case Study 3
Pressure from above

Miranda is the customer service manager in a large organisation and her employees are about to mutiny. Two weeks ago in her staff meeting, she told them that senior management was very concerned about the wages bill. Employees had to increase their number of calls. No excuses would be allowed. Productivity was the only goal.

Her employees took her remarks to heart. They processed more customer calls than ever. The number of customers' complaint calls rocketed. They complained that they weren't listened to, were cut off during mid-sentence and more. Now Miranda is saying that customer service is more important than productivity.

This morning she has announced that the quarterly report is due in a week – and that it is now top priority. Her employees don't know what is most important or where to focus their energy.

How would you advise Miranda if you were her superior?

Compare your ideas with the suggested answer on page 75.

Putting your vision into action

Up to this point, we've looked at some of the major components of leadership. Now it's time to put these concepts into some concrete steps. You may have a clear vision, but it's often difficult for employees to see its relationship to daily activities, understand their part in it, or even know how to support the vision without working at cross purposes with you.

The process for turning ideas into reality is communication, both verbal and written. Leaders are clear about the goals they set for themselves and for their followers.

Let's look first at where you stand with respect to leadership skills. Read the statements in both columns and then tick the appropriate box.

☐ I plan long-term.	☐ I focus on getting through the day or week.
☐ I determine what direction my teams should take.	☐ I wait for direction from above.
☐ I focus on how my area of responsibilty serves the organisation and our customers.	☐ I focus on what my department is supposed to do.
☐ I share my vision with employees and help to guide their work.	☐ Employees know what to do. They have their day-to-day assignments.
☐ I look at what is needed for my personal growth.	☐ I'm too busy to worry about personal growth and development.
☐ My employees are clear about how to be a success in their jobs.	☐ My employees are happy doing what they do.
☐ I consciously manage and shape change in my department.	☐ Changes occur and there is little I can do about them.
☐ I plan for the growth and development of my employees.	☐ We're too busy around here for personal growth and development.
☐ I encourage my employees to try new methods.	☐ I would prefer my employees to use the tried and true methods of doing their work.
☐ We celebrate personal and departmental successes.	☐ We keep our noses to the grindstone.

If you ticked more boxes in the left-hand column, you're on your way to becoming a leader.

Communicating a vision

Leaders generate excitement, interest and energy in others. They do this through communication. How you talk about your vision will determine how much others will want to mentally 'sign up' to follow you.

Two keys to speaking about your vision are consistency and repetition. First, let's consider consistency. If you notice, leaders are usually eager to describe their vision and do it in a rather predictable way. This isn't because they lack creativity. It is because their vision doesn't change from day to day. Leaders concentrate on how the future will look as a result of their vision. They describe the benefits inherent in their vision and their personal belief in its importance.

A vision is not a set speech given from notes on formal occasions. Rather, it appears to be impromptu and delivered to anyone who will listen. If you want others to follow you, you've got to get out there and describe where you're going. The consistency becomes important so that others will get a clear picture of where you're taking them.

Sometimes managers find communicating a vision difficult. It's more comfortable to stay in the office and do a job. That's not leadership! If you have ever heard Steve Jobs, one of the co-founders of Apple Computers, speak about his vision, you realise how infectious he can be. Jobs is very soft-spoken, but he gets people excited about the future, even if they don't understand computers.

The second part of the process is repetition. Once isn't enough. This month isn't enough. Your communication must be continuous and repetitive. Initially, people will wonder whether you are serious or if this is the 'flavour of the month'. After people hear the message frequently enough and see that your behaviour is consistent with your message then, and only then, will they begin to believe you are serious. When they know you are determined, they will also begin to believe in your vision.

An added bonus of repetition is focus. If you keep talking about your vision, you won't lose sight of the target.

Working with stakeholders

Although it is fine to communicate your vision to anyone who will listen, you will also need to target selected individuals and groups. These people are called stakeholders.

Stakeholders are those who can help or hinder you in attaining your vision because they have something at stake. Certainly this includes your employees and boss, but others are also important, such as your peers, managers of other departments, senior management, peers outside the organisation, or your family, to name just a few. On the positive side, stakeholders are people who can provide you with information, ideas, finance, a good word, or even emotional support. On the other hand, they may be individuals who see your ideas as threatening their power, security, or people who support the status quo.

If you are strategic, you need to know who these people are. Take a minute to begin jotting down some names or initials.

Likely to help   Likely to hinder

_____   _____

_____   _____

_____   _____

_____   _____

_____   _____

If some of your stakeholders are people you don't normally see in your day-to-day business, you may need to create opportunities to chat with them about your vision. These could include:

- Invite stakeholders to your departmental meeting
- Drop into their office
- Ask their advice about an idea or problem
- Take them to lunch
- Send them a book or article
- Invite them to serve on a committee

- Involve them in a planning session
- Add your own:

_____

_____

You need specific goals to reach your vision

Your vision is your picture of the future. It is global and not precise. It is critical to have a vision, but a vision alone is not enough. You also need to create specific goals to reach your vision. Goals have a more limited time horizon. Some leaders write yearly goals; others are more comfortable setting goals on a six-monthly basis. Choose whatever time limit seems most comfortable for you.

Think of your vision as where you'd like to go. Think of your goals as the specifics about how to get there. It is important to write down both visions and goals. But goals, in order to work, must have some specific built-in components.

How to write goals that work
1. Be *specific*. Identify either the exact outcome you want or the process (how much by when).
2. Make goals *measurable*. How will you measure whether you've been successful or not? Where is your goal line and how will you know if you've crossed it?
3. Goals must be *reasonable*. Sometimes in our exuberance over an idea, we set goals which are impossible to reach. Make sure your goals are humanly possible, given your present demands.
4. Finally, goals must be *time specific*. Not 'as soon as I can', but 'by 23 May'.

An important aspect of this goal-setting process is *not* to get bogged down in paperwork or write a goal for everything. Be strategic. What are the most important targets you must hit to achieve your vision? Three to five may be appropriate, never more than eight. Some examples follow.

Sample goals

Institute a customer service survey by 5 January. This survey will be posted to all our customers each quarter. The survey will enquire about: (1) quality of the product; (2) delivery time; and (3) assistance provided on the 0800 telephone number. Results from the survey will be compiled and presented at the quarterly planning meeting.

Increase our department's total sales volume by 17 per cent over last year's by the year's end. This goal ensures maintaining the present level of customer satisfaction as measured by our Customer Satisfaction Report.

Design an office layout for the new offices by 15 October. The layout will include workstations for all employees, and fulfilment space that allows for a 30 per cent addition to the present area.

Set some goals before this weekend

It is time to try writing your goals. What do you want to accomplish in the next year or sooner to move towards your vision?

My major goals are:

1. _____

2. _____

3. _____

4. _____

5. _____

Is this goal:

	Specific?	Measurable?	Reasonable	Time specific?
GOAL 1.				
2.				
3.				
4.				
5.				

Note. Goals can never be set in concrete: organisations are too dynamic. This process is your best assessment at the time, and will probably have to change to some degree during the year.

Also, you may want to involve your employees in the goal-setting process. Employees who are new to the organisation and in training may find it difficult to contribute. On the other hand, they may find it enlightening.

CHAPTER 5
Making Better and Faster Decisions

Decision-making for leaders

Once you have established a larger goal or vision, how quickly you move forward will be influenced by the decisions you make. Our success or failure is usually based on the quality of our decisions.

Four important components of leadership decisions are:

Being true to your vision: where it will take you

Your vision is your beacon, your guiding light. It underlies all your decisions and gives your leadership consistency. Employees may not agree with all your decisions, but if they see the consistency behind them, they can support and follow.

How: the formula

When we have to make dozens of decisions every day, it is very easy to 'shoot from the hip', rather than analysing the situation. A few important steps in decision-making can improve your product and/or service.

When: analysis paralysis

The information age has brought thousands of facts to our fingertips. You might think this leads to a better decision, but the opposite is often the case. The sheer amount of data can lead to analysis paralysis. Leaders must know how to make decisions without poring over every bit of data.

Who: decisions at the right level

Nothing can bog a leader down more quickly than trying to make all the decisions. It is not easy to delegate decisions to others who might not be as knowledgeable. And it can be confusing to trace which decisions are yours. Most important in delegating decisions is strategically choosing which to delegate and then consistently delegating those to others.

Using a formula for decision-making

Some decisions are simple and the answers are obvious. Others are complex and require you to weigh a variety of factors. At times, it's not even clear what problems or issues have to be solved.

Having a formula to help you to sort out a decision can help you to look at factors and identify your best options.

The formula below is designed to help render decision-making more methodical.

Process	Instructions
1. Define desired outcome.	You need to know exactly what you want to accomplish before you can decide the best way to do it.
2. Establish decision criteria.	What are the guidelines? For example, if you were deciding whether to drive or take the bus to work, you would consider factors such as cost, time saved, or safety.
3. Propose alternative solutions.	Write out all possible courses of action that will lead to the desired outcome.
4. Investigate – get all possible facts.	Accumulate as many facts as time permits. List them on a separate sheet of paper.

Process	Instructions
5. Settle on the top three choices.	List them.
6. Instigate a comparison.	Weigh the three choices and decide between them. Consult others if necessary.
7. Opt for the best choice.	List your final decision.
8. Notify those involved decisively.	The way you articulate your decision can be as important as the quality of the decision itself. Write out how you intend to announce it.
9. See that decision is fully implemented.	A good decision must be made to work. Write out how you intend to do this.

Knowing when to hold and when to fold

Timing is another significant element in your leadership tool kit. Obviously, you want to make the best possible decision in the most efficient way. Some managers demand all the financial data, historical information, power-brokers' opinions, customer feedback and more. Unfortunately, by the time all this data is gathered, it is either too late or overwhelming. The results are inconsistent. This type of situation leads to poor decisions at best and paralysis at worst.

So how do you make decisions if you can't know everything? First, as a leader, you must keep up to date and informed on the trends in your industry, organisation and/or department. You need to look for patterns of growth, opportunities and problems. Leaders are continuously working to anticipate the future rather than react to it. Certainly there may be some data you must have or some individuals (such as your boss) whose support is absolutely necessary. But the challenge of leadership is judging when you have enough information so you are not shooting from the hip, and not waiting so long that the strategic moment to take advantage of the situation has passed. Leaders often talk about making 'gut' decisions. Although this may sound unusual, what they are really talking about is understanding the patterns without getting lost in the data.

A reality of decision-making is that you will at times make the wrong decision. Yes, if you had waited longer, this would have become obvious. Consider it a lesson in your school of leadership. You won't do it perfectly every time. Fifty-one per cent of making the right decision is a step in the right direction.

Freeing yourself to lead

The 'who' of decision-making is an essential factor. You can't be a true leader sensing the environment for trends and concentrating on the long haul if you are bogged down in the daily detail of decision-making. If employees need to bring everything to you for approval, the decision-making process must be pushed to a lower level.

Consider how many decisions, large and small, you make in a day. Could or should others be shouldering part of this load? Often managers are reluctant to let go of decision-making. Following are some of the common reasons. Tick those you feel are true of you.

☐ I can decide faster.

☐ I would not be in control if I'm not making the decisions.

☐ I know all the factors; my employees don't.

☐ The employee might make a mistake.

☐ I have more experience and therefore can make better decisions.

☐ I feel guilty asking the employee to make the decision when it's my responsibility.

☐ My employees don't like making decisions and want me to decide.

☐ I like making all the decisions.

If any of these sound like you, it's time to change. You can't be a leader if you are involved in every day-to-day decision. If you feel your employees are unprepared to handle decisions on their own, then it is time to prepare them. If they don't have the background, make sure they get it. If they don't have the confidence, work with them. Praise their good decisions. If they tend to put it back on your plate, consistently give the decision back. Leaders cannot be involved in the daily load of details.

Where you must focus your decision-making energy is on those issues that set the direction of your responsibilities. You must be at the forefront in any decision that will have a long-term impact.

Case Study 4
Charles can't decide

Charles dreamed of the day he would become a manager. He looked forward to running the show and making the decisions. Charles and his company enjoy a sophisticated management information system that can provide reports, data, projections, and the history of just about every product imaginable to help him make the right decisions.

Much to his surprise, Charles finds his stomach in knots when it's time to decide. He wonders if there is another way to look at the data. Should he ask for an additional report? Should he talk to accounts? Should he do more research? Should he read another article? He wants to make the right decision and suddenly it seems as if there is no right decision.

Lately, Charles has noticed that his employees seem to be kidding him about whether decisions have been made yet. Even his boss has made some remarks. The problem is, he's just not sure yet if there are other factors to be considered.

What would you advise Charles to do? See authors' response on page 75.

PORTRAIT OF A DECISION

You may remember the Tylenol poisoning scare that happened several years ago. People who had taken Tylenol were dying and no one knew why. James Burke, the Chief Executive Officer of Johnson & Johnson, faced one of the toughest decisions of his life. Should he pull Tylenol from all the shops?

The financial cost would be enormous. The legal implications could be staggering. His decision was – pull the product.

Burke attributes his decision to the values underlying his company, Johnson & Johnson's credo which begins, 'We believe our first responsibility is to the doctors, nurses and patients, to mothers and all others who use our products and services.' Burke is a clear example of a leader who knew his values and used them to make decisions. Additionally, he kept the long view in mind. Yes, J&J suffered financially that year, but they came back stronger than ever with more customer trust than they could have bought with millions spent in advertising.

Developing your decision-making skills

Read the statement at both sides of the scale and then circle the number that best indicates where you belong.

	High	**Low**	
When making an important decision I consider how it fits my vision.	10 9 8 7 6 5 4 3 2 1		It's too difficult to consider my vision when making important decisions.
My followers see consistency in my decisions.	10 9 8 7 6 5 4 3 2 1		There's very little consistency in my decisions.
I feel comfortable making a decision without all related data.	10 9 8 7 6 5 4 3 2 1		I must have as much data as possible to make a decision.
I am careful not to overwhelm myself with information when making a decision.	10 9 8 7 6 5 4 3 2 1		I often feel overwhelmed by the data when making a decision.
I am able to make quicker decisions.	10 9 8 7 6 5 4 3 2 1		I procrastinate when decisions are important.
I communicate my decision to those who will be affected.	10 9 8 7 6 5 4 3 2 1		I neglect or forget to tell people about decisions that may affect them.
I stay up to date with industry and organisation trends.	10 9 8 7 6 5 4 3 2 1		I'm too busy to worry about industry and organisation trends.
I delegate appropriate decisions to employees.	10 9 8 7 6 5 4 3 2 1		I make most of the decisions.

	High	Low
I am committed to developing my employees so they can make more and better decisions.	10 9 8 7 6 5 4 3 2 1	My employees would prefer me to make the decisions.
When a decision is complex, I follow a logical formula.	10 9 8 7 6 5 4 3 2 1	When a decision is complex, I muddle through as best I can.

SCORE ☐

If you scored 100–90, you are an outstanding decision-maker on all important fronts. If you scored 89–80, you are very good at decision-making and involve the appropriate individuals. If you scored 79–70, you are doing well, but may want to look at the answers you ticked for areas you can improve on even more. If you scored below 70, you may want to develop a decision-making improvement plan.

Taking care of your personal growth

A serious oversight some managers make is not attending to their personal leadership growth. Just as with developing employees, what you know and do today won't be sufficient for the rapidly changing business environment. You can't let personal growth slide until you 'have the time'. That time will never come. You must have a development plan for yourself. If you don't write it down, another 'crisis' will take priority. Take a moment to assess your development needs and then take appropriate action.

What I need to know	How I'm going to learn it	By when?
(For example: the latest trends in my industry	Attend an association meeting at which an industry forecaster is speaking.	December 19 ____)

Helping your staff to grow

People normally fall into two groups: those who create their future, and those who let others create it. Leaders are solidly in the former group.

Leaders are never satisfied with the status quo. They are always looking for ways to 'do things better than we are doing them today'. True leaders seem to brim with new ideas. These ideas come from constant scanning of the environment for trends and direction. But the focus on improvement isn't just products or services – it's also the people.

As a leader, your important message to your followers is that everyone, regardless of experience or job title, should be constantly improving. Daily work becomes a continuous education. Some ways to foster personal improvement include:

- Attend formal outside workshops and seminars.
- Work directly with employees to share insights.
- Devise group projects for cross training.
- Visit other organisations or departments.
- Develop or attend in-house training courses.
- Encourage special projects which enhance skills and abilities.
- Read books, journals and articles.

One company chairman holds a monthly book review meeting with her key managers. The chairman selects one book a month related to business. All read the book and then discuss which ideas are appropriate for their business.

Whatever avenue you use, the message you send when you encourage growth is that you encourage people to expand their skills and knowledge.

CHAPTER 6
Taking More Risks

The million-pound flop

The chairman of Acme Manufacturing phoned and asked to see Bob. Bob knows why the chairman rang and wonders if it is time to update his CV.

Bob is the manager of new product development. For the past year he has been working on a special product. So far the company has spent more than a million pounds in the development, production and preliminary marketing of this new product.

The product has been on the market for three months and first quarter sales have just been reported. The product appears to be a total flop with no hope of selling anywhere near its projection. That's a million pounds down the drain and Bob was one of those primarily responsible.

Bob entered the chairman's office fearing it would be the end of his career at Acme. Although he contributed a lot to the company over the years, a million pounds is a million pounds. To speed things along, Bob told the chairman, 'I know why you asked to see me. I understand your position. You'll have my resignation by the end of the day.'

The chairman interrupted Bob by saying, 'Slow down. We all have to make educated guesses when making decisions. I'm sure you learned a lot from this product launch. I can't afford to lose you. We just spent a million pounds on your education.'

1. What do you think the chairman gained from this approach?
2. How do you think this will affect Bob's future performance?

Learning from failures

Whenever we change how we do things, expect some problems. Whenever we make a change, we are taking a risk. This is not necessarily bad; in fact, progress comes from applying new ideas to old problems. Leaders are risk takers. As they forge into the unknown looking for a better way, they may stumble, meet a roadblock or fail.

As a leader, you obviously don't want to take unwarranted risks. But it would be far more damaging to take no risks. Calculated risks are part and parcel of leadership.

What is important is how you deal with your failure should one of your risks backfire. Some managers allow failure to damage their self-esteem. As a result, these individuals are less likely to take future risks and the process can become a downward career spiral. Managers who only do what is safe will not become leaders. The focus during failure needs to be on what has been learned. Leaders see risk taking and failure as an opportunity to learn valuable lessons.

List three failures resulting from risks you took and write what you learned from each experience. Use more paper if necessary.

Failure	Lessons learned
1.	1.
2.	2.
3.	3.

Were these failures valuable learning experiences for you?

YES ☐   NO ☐

Risk analysis exercise

Often we are reluctant to take a risk because of various imagined negative consequences. But we are usually vague about what those consequences actually would be. If we realistically identify the worst possible outcome, it isn't all that bad.

To overcome this, you might try the following exercise. You can do this with a risk you are considering or one that one of your employees is reluctant to try.

Step 1. Describe the potential risk: _____

_____

_____

_____

Step 2. Describe the worst possible outcome.
(*Note.* Be specific. Not 'It would be just awful', or 'I'd look like a fool', but 'The report would be a day late', or 'Sue would think I hadn't tried.')

_____

_____

_____

_____

Step 3. Now list the benefits if the risk is a success.

_____

_____

_____

_____

_____

Step 4. On balance, is it worth taking the risk? ____ Yes ____ No

Leaders can effectively manage change

As your vision takes shape on the job, things will naturally begin to change. Most of us are to some degree uncomfortable with change. Some recognise the benefit of doing business differently and take advantage of opportunities. At the other extreme, others will wail, 'We tried that back in '82 and it doesn't work!'

As a leader, when you encounter resistance, you must manage change strategically. To assist you, there are three major tools in your 'change management tool kit'. They are: reward, comfort in the new way, and replay optimism. Following are the three primary ways to deal with the resistance to change you will inevitably encounter.

1. Providing pay-offs

Pay-offs or rewards can be extremely effective in bringing about change. Given the change you would like followers to master, what pay-offs can you provide when the change occurs? How can you make it rewarding when your follower takes the risk of trying something new? You can't wait until followers are 100 per cent behind the change; they may never get there. Instead, when you see an employee begin to accept the change, you need to praise and acknowledge the attempt, even if it's not whole-hearted or done perfectly. What this means is, you are providing a pay-off to make it worth going through the change.

2. Greasing the skids

The second tool is to make change more comfortable. How can you make the status quo so undesirable that the employee would prefer to make the change? You may change things so that it takes more time or effort to do it the old way. Or you might remove approval or other social awards that the employee previously received. Often group pressure, such as joking or teasing, can help some of the most entrenched to change old ways.

3. Assuring with optimism

Some people are extremely fearful of change. They can only see the down side. As a leader you need to help such a person see the benefits of the change. You can do this with reassuring optimism. You should consistently state your belief in the worth, impact, possibility, etc, of the change. You don't let the change resisters pull you down with their negativity. If the resister says, 'Top management will never support it', the optimistic reply is, 'I think once we've presented our ideas, they will be behind us.' State what you plan to gain the needed support.

Let's look at a case study.

Change exercise

Neil, one of your employees, is responsible for putting together the company's monthly newsletter. This takes a large part of his time and Neil is justly very proud of his product. Virtually everyone in the company knows Neil because of the newsletter, and he's often acknowledged formally and informally because he does such a good job.

Recently, you've become aware of desktop publishing. After seeing a demonstration, you couldn't wait to tell Neil about the possibilities. When you told Neil about it, he immediately threw up verbal barriers. He said using a computer instead of doing everything by hand would take away the creative process which now makes the newsletter so outstanding.

What could you do in each of these areas? (List your responses below.)

Providing pay-offs. _____

_____

_____

_____

_____

Greasing the skids. _____

_____

_____

_____

_____

Assuring with optimism. _____

_____

_____

_____

_____

Compare your responses with those of the authors below. Your responses do not have to be identical with those of the authors, but should convey the same spirit.

Compare your response
Author suggested responses:

Providing pay-offs
(a) If Neil uses the computer for part of the newsletter, praise him.
(b) Offer him the opportunity to attend a desktop publishing seminar.
(c) Discuss with him the opportunities to link up with others, such as graphics specialists, to obtain more and better input for the newsletters.
(d) Mention any positive feedback you have heard about his attempts at new or different techniques.
(e) Identify newsletters he admires from other organisations and have him visit those organisations, in company time, to research the techniques they are using.

Greasing the skids
(a) Move Neil's layout equipment to the back room and put the computer in its place.
(b) Stop commenting on the newsletter.
(c) Create performance goals related to automation of the newsletter.
(d) Give him an assignment that would more easily or professionally be done with desktop publishing.
(e) Limit the amount of time he can spend on the newsletter.
(f) Introduce others in the organisation to desktop publishing so they question Neil about his expertise in this area.

Assuring with optimism
State your beliefs about:

(a) The professional new look desktop publishing will give the newsletter.
(b) Neil's ability to transfer to desktop publishing.
(c) The support you've had from top management.

(In general, when Neil comments on why it won't work, you state your belief about how it will work.)

The safe road to nowhere

How you handle the failures of followers is as important as how you handle personal failures. So often, a manager will cajole, coax and beg a follower to be creative and experiment with new methods. They see employee resistance simply as stubbornness. What this manager may fail to take into account is that in the past, when the followers *did* try something new and it failed, the follower had a negative experience from the manager. This type of experience encourages taking the safe road in the future.

An example of a typical change-frustration was an executive who managed 30 service businesses in five countries. He once said about the managers running the businesses, 'I keep talking to them about needing to change but nothing changes. Sometimes I just want to shake them.' What this executive failed to take into account was that unsuccessful change attempts in the past had brought swift negative responses from head office. What the executive saw as good management on his part, his managers saw as a problem. His people weren't stupid, they were simply protecting themselves.

If you want change, you cannot punish reasonable risks. You may even want to reward a failure if the risk was well conceived and one to be admired. If you let your employees know that you understand the rationale for doing what was done and that you appreciate his or her effort, you will probably have two results: (1) a surprised employee; and (2) someone ready to risk change in the future.

CHAPTER 7
Summary

Management/leadership assessment scale

This survey describes 20 practices that are commonly demonstrated by excellent managers and 20 commonly demonstrated by effective leaders. Read all the statements carefully. Then decide as a manager/leader the priority you would assign to each practice or characteristic. Indicate your decision by circling the appropriate number.

	PRIORITY				
	Highest	**High**	**Important**	**Modest**	**Low**
1. Gets tough when needed.	5	4	3	2	1
2. Speaks well to groups.	5	4	3	2	1
3. Establishes a consistent, clear discipline line.	5	4	3	2	1
4. Attracts others to message that is given.	5	4	3	2	1
5. Provides environment conducive to a feeling of cohesiveness.	5	4	3	2	1
6. Communicates sense of being in charge.	5	4	3	2	1
7. Has full backing from those reporting to her/him.	5	4	3	2	1
8. Converts employees into followers.	5	4	3	2	1

	PRIORITY				
	Highest	High	Important	Modest	Low
9. Strives to win by allowing employees also to win.	5	4	3	2	1
10. Attracts others to join his/her group.	5	4	3	2	1
11. Provides important rewards for staff.	5	4	3	2	1
12. Uses sources of power in a sensitive, consistent manner.	5	4	3	2	1
13. Shows compassion.	5	4	3	2	1
14. Strong track record for making solid and decisive decisions.	5	4	3	2	1
15. Good listener.	5	4	3	2	1
16. Formalises and 'stages' communication announcements.	5	4	3	2	1
17. Expresses thoughts clearly.	5	4	3	2	1
18. Prudent risk taker.	5	4	3	2	1
19. Keeps employees fully informed.	5	4	3	2	1
20. Articulates an inspiring mission.	5	4	3	2	1
21. Highly ethical.	5	4	3	2	1
22. Generates a feeling of pride in followers.	5	4	3	2	1
23. Delegates effectively.	5	4	3	2	1
24. Ties short-term work goals to mission.	5	4	3	2	1
25. Shares large and small victories with staff.	5	4	3	2	1
26. Gets others caught up in his/her positive force.	5	4	3	2	1

	PRIORITY				
	Highest	High	Important	Modest	Low
27. Makes work enjoyable.	5	4	3	2	1
28. Creates active tempo.	5	4	3	2	1
29. Maintains positive, upbeat attitude.	5	4	3	2	1
30. Highly energetic; not desk-bound.	5	4	3	2	1
31. Admits to mistakes.	5	4	3	2	1
32. Good negotiator; knows when to compromise.	5	4	3	2	1
33. Follows logical steps in making decisions.	5	4	3	2	1
34. If she/he resigned, others would consider following.	5	4	3	2	1
35. Consults others in making decisions.	5	4	3	2	1
36. Builds commitment to his/her cause.	5	4	3	2	1
37. Uses management role with sensitivity.	5	4	3	2	1
38. Stands firm on principle.	5	4	3	2	1
39. Respected by employees when authority is used.	5	4	3	2	1
40. Communicates a power image.	5	4	3	2	1

Now complete the box overleaf.

All the practices that are found in effective *managers* have odd numbers. Those practices not always found in managers but *usually found in leaders* have even numbers.

Please add up all the numbers you circled in the *odd* numbered statements and enter them in this box:

Management
practices

Please add up all the numbers you circled in the *even* numbered statements and enter them in this box:

Leadership
practices

Possible interpretation

1. If the score in the management practices box above is higher than the score on page 21, it is an indication that becoming more familiar with leadership practices may improve your status as a manager either now or later.
2. If the score in the leadership practices box is 80 or above, it would appear you are getting a signal that you are 'ready' to take on a stronger leadership role.
3. If the score in the leadership practices box is between 60 and 80, it may be a signal that you are 'getting ready' to move into a leadership role.
4. If your leadership practices score is substantially less than your management practices score, it may be an indication that leadership, at this time, may not be for you.
5. Please list any additional interpretations that you make from the results of your assessments.

_____

_____

_____

_____

Monday's reality

A leadership maintenance kit

Like having your car serviced regularly, the purpose of this one-page kit is to remind you to do maintenance on your leadership skills. Tick those that need to be activated on Monday morning.

- ☐ Keep alive the 'positive force' created last week?

- ☐ Give new rewards to staff?

- ☐ Solve any carry-over problems decisively?

- ☐ Restore the vision previously painted?

- ☐ Be a better example than last week?

- ☐ Establish a more upbeat tempo?

- ☐ Laugh at yourself more frequently?

- ☐ Keep management skills sharp so you will continue to have more time to lead?

- ☐ Make others feel better about their decision to follow you?

- ☐ Make better use of power sources?

- ☐ Do a better job of holding emotions in check?

- ☐ Communicate a stronger, more positive attitude?

- ☐ If goals are met by Thursday, relax with staff and share the victory on Friday?

- ☐ Spend more time teaching others?

- ☐ Show a stronger bearing through the way you walk, talk and listen?

- ☐ Take more risks?

- ☐ Make faster, better decisions?

Developing your leadership skills

If you've chosen to develop your leadership skills, you probably have a number of specific skills you feel are important to strengthen. As we've mentioned, it's often easy to get caught up in daily crises and lose sight of long-term objectives.

Take a few minutes right now to do some planning for your own leadership development. What area(s) would you like to focus on developing in the next two to three months?

☐	Personality power	☐	Managing change
☐	My vision	☐	Developing stakeholders
☐	Speaking skills	☐	Long-term goal setting
☐	Delegation	☐	Decision-making
☐	Risk taking	☐	Other

Developing your leadership vision

A true leader is constantly developing his or her skills. You have probably identified some leadership skills you would like to develop. You may wonder where to begin. A good idea is first to list the skills you wish to improve. Then prioritise which you plan to attack first (give these an 'A'). Those that are important but not top priority should be labelled 'B'. Any remaining can be labelled 'C'.

Leadership tools to develop

The second step in this process is to identify a few leaders you feel are top-notch models, and whom you have an opportunity to observe.

Leaders to observe

The next step is to make a conscious effort to observe these leaders and how they use the tools you are developing. Even better is to pick their brains and get some leadership coaching.

Ideas from leaders

The final step is to create your own model of leadership. What are the qualities you feel are critical in order to be the best leader you can possibly be?

My leadership model

Case Study 5
Robin gets ready to lead

Robin has been a supervisor for six months. She has become a good administrator, and does what is required of her in the position.

Recently, Robin has been reading about leadership and found herself admiring individuals with these qualities. As Robin began to consider developing her own leadership abilities, she realised that such an endeavour would not be easy. She would have to take a hard look at her strengths and weaknesses and really put some work into self-development.

Robin is torn. The position only 'requires' that she be effective in her administrative duties, which won't necessitate any additional work on her part. However, Robin also sees an opportunity to make a difference as a leader, but that's going to require some real commitment to her own development.

Which choice is right for Robin? Compare your answer with that of the authors on page 75.

Answers to case studies

Case Study 1
Crystal made a smart move in switching role models. Some organisations develop many good managers but few leaders. In these firms, managers usually stay in their present positions longer. In almost all organisations, leadership is the key to greater upward mobility.

Case Study 2
Barbara's dilemma is far more common than she realises. Employees who receive many accolades for meticulously taking care of details find the move to management and leadership exceptionally painful. It is time for Barbara to reassess her position. She needs to develop her vision and long-term goals.

She needs to see the patterns and trends in her department, organisation and industry. If she stays in her world of detail (her choice) her upward mobility is limited.

Case Study 3

Miranda, confused by senior management, is sending mixed signals to her staff. As a result, they are frustrated and critical of her leadership. Miranda needs to give her followers one clear, understandable direction even if this means acting as a 'buffer and interpreter' of what she is receiving from above.

Case Study 4

Charles needs to design a decision-making formula that is comfortable for him to use – one in which he can have confidence. After doing this, he needs to remind himself that: (1) All decisions are calculated risks; (2) Decisions can usually be reversed without damage to the image of the leader; (3) Nobody is maintaining a decision 'track record' on Charles; (4) Making no decision can be the worst decision of all.

Case Study 5

Robin does not appear to be 'ready' to make a commitment to leadership preparation. It could be suggested to her that another year of management preparation (taking courses at night) could help her to build a better base from which she could launch her leadership talents at a later date. Robin will not be free to lead until her management skills reach a higher level.

Further Reading from Kogan Page

How to Lead – So Others Follow Willingly, James L Lundy, 1990
Leadership Skills for Women, Marilyn Manning and Patricia
    Haddock, 1989
Not Bosses But Leaders, John Adair, 1988

Better Management Skills series

Creative Thinking in Business
Delegating for Results
Effective Employee Participation
Effective Meeting Skills
*Effective Performance Appraisals**
Effective Presentation Skills
*How to Communicate Effectively**
*How to Develop a Positive Attitude**
How to Develop Assertiveness
*How to Motivate People**
Improving Relations at Work
Make Every Minute Count
Managing Disagreement Constructively
Managing Organisational Change
Managing Quality Customer Service
Project Management
Risk Taking
Successful Negotiation

* Also available on cassette.

Learning to Lead

Systematic Problem-Solving and Decision-Making
Team Building

A full list of books for managers, published by Kogan Page, is available from the publishers at 120 Pentonville Road, London N1 9JN; telephone 071-278 0433; fax 071-837 6348.